Choose
Grace

Choose Grace

A JOURNAL FOR NOT BEING SO HARD
ON YOURSELF (AND OTHERS, TOO!)

DRIVEN

Published in the United States by Driven, an imprint of Zeitgeist™,
a division of Penguin Random House LLC, New York.

penguinrandomhouse.com

ISBN: 9780525617730

Written by L.J. Tracosas
Book design by Rachel Marek

Printed in the United States of America

10 9 8 7 6 5 4 3 2 1

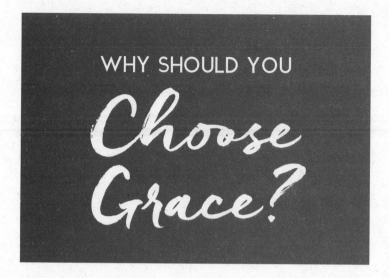

WHY SHOULD YOU *Choose Grace?*

Grace can be hard to define. It's a feeling and a mindset. It's something taken, and it's something given. You can create it, and you can destroy it.

Kindness, forgiveness, leeway, empathy, positivity—these help foster grace. Doubt, rigidity, and negativity destroy it.

We are often the most unkind to ourselves. Negative self-talk perpetuates stress, anxiety, depression, and worse. Perfectionism ensures that we're unhappy and unmotivated. Turning in on ourselves prevents us from connecting with others.

But choosing grace—for ourselves and for others—can help. What if instead of focusing on insecurities and doubt, you choose to compliment and trust yourself? Instead of hating your imperfections, you choose to accept them? What if instead of telling yourself you could do better, you choose to tell yourself you're doing a great job?

Being kinder to ourselves helps us be better to the people around us—and being better to the people around us
helps us feel better about ourselves, too. Being more open,
accepting, and forgiving toward yourself and others gives
you a wider world where more is possible.

The journaling prompts in this book will inspire you to
encourage yourself and others. They'll help you focus on
the positive, combat the negative, and cultivate peace of
mind.

"Grace is not part
of consciousness; it
is the amount of
light in our souls."

—Pope Francis

Let's start with a simple question: What does grace mean to you?

_____

_____

_____

_____

_____

_____

_____

_____

_____

_____

_____

_____

_____

_____

_____

_____

_____

_____

_____

_____

_____

_____

_____

_____

Write about a time where you felt grace in the way that you described it on the previous page. What happened? Did someone extend grace to you, or did you offer it to someone else?

Negative self-talk is one way that we can rob ourselves of happiness.

Practice giving yourself some grace. Write down three statements that you know you say to yourself. How can you rephrase them to be kinder to yourself? Fill in the blanks following the example.

NEGATIVE SELF-TALK: _I messed up my presentation today. I'm so stupid._

CHOOSING GRACE: _I made a mistake today. It happens; everyone is human._

NEGATIVE SELF-TALK: _____

CHOOSING GRACE: _____

NEGATIVE SELF-TALK: _____

CHOOSING GRACE: _____

NEGATIVE SELF-TALK: _____

_____

_____

_____

_____

CHOOSING GRACE: _____

_____

_____

_____

_____

NEGATIVE SELF-TALK: _____

_____

_____

_____

_____

CHOOSING GRACE: _____

_____

_____

_____

_____

NEGATIVE SELF-TALK: _____

_____

_____

_____

_____

CHOOSING GRACE: _____

_____

_____

_____

Everyone has cringeworthy moments they find themselves replaying over and over in their minds.

That embarrassing typo in an email, the awkward way you said hello to your neighbor, that joke you made that didn't land—at all... Free your mind by writing about your moments here and leaving it all on the page.

Doubts. Everyone has them.

On one hand, it's healthy to double-check your decisions and make sure you've really thought them through. On the other hand, doubt can affect your confidence and prevent you from fully enjoying life. List some decisions you've made that you have doubts about—and boost your confidence by writing how well your decisions will play out.

DOUBT: _____

_____

_____

_____

_____

_____

_____

_____

CONFIDENCE BOOSTER: _____

_____

_____

_____

_____

_____

_____

_____

_____

_____

_____

DOUBT: _____

_____

_____

_____

_____

_____

CONFIDENCE BOOSTER: _____

_____

_____

_____

_____

_____

_____

DOUBT: _____

_____

_____

_____

_____

CONFIDENCE BOOSTER: _____

_____

_____

_____

_____

_____

What's worrying you right now?

Jot everything down here. Allow the thoughts to come freely, and then let them stay in this book. Don't carry your worries with you today.

_____

_____

_____

_____

_____

_____

_____

_____

_____

_____

_____

_____

_____

_____

_____

_____

_____

_____

_____

_____

_____

_____

"Worry often gives
a small thing a
big shadow."

—Proverb

Grace can be most apparent in the worst times—against the backdrop of loss, ruin, sadness, and devastation, its light shines most bright.

Think back on some of the harder moments in your life. In what ways did grace reveal itself to you?

_____

_____

_____

_____

_____

_____

_____

_____

_____

_____

_____

_____

_____

_____

_____

_____

_____

_____

_____

_____

_____

_____

Expectation doesn't always equal reality.

When was the last time a conversation, project, or event didn't pan out the way you'd envisioned? Try to identify one to three positive outcomes that occurred, even if the overall experience fell short of your aspirations.

EXPECTATION: _____

_____

_____

_____

REALITY: _____

_____

_____

_____

POSITIVE OUTCOMES:

1. _____

_____

2. _____

_____

3. _____

_____

EXPECTATION: _____

_____

_____

_____

_____

REALITY: _____
_____
_____
_____

POSITIVE OUTCOMES:

1. _____
_____

2. _____
_____

3. _____
_____
_____

EXPECTATION: _____
_____
_____
_____

REALITY: _____
_____
_____
_____

POSITIVE OUTCOMES:

1. _____
_____

2. _____
_____

3. _____
_____
_____

Believe it or not, someone would be *really* impressed with everything you've achieved so far in your life. YOU!

Imagine your younger self is meeting you today. Write yourself a short letter from the perspective of younger you. Which aspects of your present life would your past self be most proud of? Why?

"When grace is joined with wrinkles, it is adorable."

—Victor Hugo

We are our own harshest critics.

Write down three things that have happened recently that you wished you had handled differently. Then, imagine these three events happening to someone you care about. What advice would you give them? How does it differ from what you'd tell yourself in the same scenario?

1. WHAT HAPPENED: _____
_____
_____
_____
_____
_____
_____
_____
_____
_____

KIND ADVICE: _____
_____
_____
_____
_____
_____
_____
_____
_____
_____
_____
_____

2. WHAT HAPPENED: _____

_____

_____

_____

_____

_____

_____

KIND ADVICE: _____

_____

_____

_____

_____

_____

_____

3. WHAT HAPPENED: _____

_____

_____

_____

_____

_____

_____

KIND ADVICE: _____

_____

_____

_____

_____

Focus on someone else for a few minutes.

Call a friend, interview your child, or have a conversation with a partner. Write down their answers to these questions.

PERSON INTERVIEWED: _____

_____

WHAT MADE YOU SMILE TODAY? _____

_____

_____

_____

_____

_____

_____

_____

_____

_____

_____

_____

_____

_____

_____

_____

_____

_____

WHAT CHALLENGED YOU TODAY? _____

_____

_____

_____

_____

_____

_____

_____

_____

WHAT DID YOU DO FOR YOURSELF TODAY? _____

_____

_____

_____

_____

_____

_____

_____

_____

WHAT DID YOU DO TO HELP ANOTHER PERSON TODAY? _____

_____

_____

_____

_____

_____

_____

_____

Center yourself with a mantra.

When life feels out of control and your inner monologue is turning terrible, speaking a positive phrase (to yourself or aloud) can help you come back to square one. Draft a few go-to mantras here. Some examples might be: I will meet the moment as it comes. I can handle anything.

"Kind words can be short and easy to speak, but their echoes are truly endless."

—Mother Teresa

Grace can be a state of mind that you can nurture and strengthen. Tools like meditation and journaling are just two grace-focused practices.

How do you tap into grace when you need it most? How can you cultivate a mindset of grace daily?

Write about something that happened this week that you have not been able to stop replaying in your mind.

What about it is causing you anxiety? How can you flip the narrative to see the situation from a different point of view?

_____

_____

_____

_____

_____

_____

_____

_____

_____

_____

_____

_____

_____

_____

_____

_____

_____

_____

_____

_____

Gratitude and grace often go hand in hand.

Write down ten small things you are grateful for today.

1. _____

   _____

2. _____

   _____

   _____

3. _____

   _____

4. _____

   _____

   _____

5. _____

   _____

6. _____

   _____

   _____

7. _____

   _____

8. _____

   _____

   _____

9. _____

   _____

10. _____

   _____

"Gratitude is riches."

—Doris Day

When we work to cultivate our own grace, it becomes something that we can share with others.

Is there someone in your life who needs grace right now? Who is it, and why are they in need? What can you do for them?

WHO NEEDS HELP: _____

_____

_____

_____

WHAT ARE THEY DEALING WITH: _____

_____

_____

_____

_____

_____

_____

_____

_____

_____

_____

_____

_____

_____

_____

_____

_____

WHAT I CAN DO: _____

_____
_____
_____
_____
_____
_____
_____
_____
_____
_____
_____
_____
_____
_____
_____
_____
_____
_____
_____
_____
_____
_____
_____
_____
_____

When was the last time you checked in on a friend without asking for anything in return?

Reflect on this gesture and how it made you feel. If you can't recall an example, what do you think is stopping you from reaching out?

Sometimes people show each other grace in little ways.

Quietly handling a household chore for your partner. Taking in a neighbor's garbage can after trash day. Holding the door open for a stranger. What are some little things that people have done for you?

_____
_____
_____
_____
_____
_____
_____
_____
_____
_____
_____
_____
_____
_____
_____
_____
_____
_____
_____
_____

List three actions you can take to show people around you grace this week.

1. _____
   _____
   _____
   _____
   _____
   _____
   _____
   _____

2. _____
   _____
   _____
   _____
   _____
   _____
   _____
   _____

3. _____
   _____
   _____
   _____
   _____
   _____
   _____

Being fully present—with yourself and others—in the moment is a gift.

Think about a time when someone was really, truly present with you. What did that feel like?

_____

_____

_____

_____

_____

_____

_____

_____

_____

_____

_____

_____

_____

_____

_____

_____

_____

_____

_____

_____

_____

How can you do that for someone else?

_____
_____
_____
_____
_____
_____
_____
_____
_____
_____
_____
_____
_____
_____
_____
_____
_____
_____
_____
_____
_____
_____
_____
_____
_____

Sometimes, the people we're closest to can disappoint us despite their best efforts.

Think about the last time a friend, colleague, or partner let you down. Was it really their intention to hurt you, or might they have made a mistake? Did they express regret? It's OK to feel disappointed. Write about their actions and the feelings they triggered.

How does it feel to express yourself?

Changing our point of view and thinking outside of ourselves can help us extend grace to others.

Think about a terse or testy interaction you've had at home or at work lately. Could there be an underlying, unrelated issue creating tension? How can you start with kindness the next time you have this interaction?

"Be kind whenever possible. It is always possible."

—Dalai Lama

Sometimes to preserve your peace of mind you need space.

Taking a time-out, a moment to yourself, a period away helps you keep calm and kind. How can you create this essential space for yourself?

_____

_____

_____

_____

_____

_____

_____

_____

_____

_____

_____

_____

_____

_____

_____

_____

_____

_____

_____

In the same way that you need space for yourself to cultivate grace, others do, too.

What can you do to help create space for the people closest to you?

PERSON 1: _____

_____

_____

_____

_____

_____

_____

_____

_____

_____

_____

_____

_____

_____

_____

_____

_____

_____

_____

_____

_____

_____

PERSON 2: _____

Is there something you've done that you feel sorry for, but—maybe because of pride, maybe because of embarrassment—you haven't apologized for?

Express your true regrets here.

What's stopping you from saying this to the person or people you feel you've wronged?

_____

_____

_____

_____

_____

_____

_____

_____

_____

_____

_____

_____

_____

_____

_____

_____

_____

_____

_____

_____

_____

_____

Let's face it: People can be rude, abrupt, and nasty to one another.

It can be tempting to respond in kind—even a hint of disrespect (perceived or real) can make tempers flare. Describe a time when someone treated you unkindly. Maybe it was a stranger at the store or someone in your family. What happened? How did you respond to them?

It can be very difficult to remember grace in trying moments when emotions are high—but it's the most important time to do so. Think back on the incident. How could you have responded differently?

_____

_____

_____

_____

_____

_____

_____

_____

_____

_____

_____

_____

_____

_____

_____

_____

_____

_____

_____

_____

_____

_____

Is there someone in your life who is a source of negativity?

Maybe you have an otherwise wonderful coworker, but she constantly complains about her job. Or your friend is in a rut and has nothing nice to say about anyone when you call to catch up. How can you help them be more positive? Write down how this conversation might go.

_____

_____

_____

_____

_____

_____

_____

_____

_____

_____

_____

_____

_____

_____

_____

_____

_____

_____

Are you carrying anger or a grudge?

People can hurt us deeply, and carrying that pain can mani-
fest itself in destructive ways like resentment and bitterness.
Write about what happened and how it made you feel.

Can you forgive the person who hurt you?

What do you need for that to happen?

_____

_____

_____

_____

_____

_____

_____

_____

_____

_____

_____

_____

_____

_____

_____

_____

_____

_____

_____

_____

_____

_____

_____

_____

Sometimes, the person we're angry at is ourselves. We can let ourselves down or act against our own principles.

Can you forgive yourself? Write an apology letter to yourself here.

"To err is human;
to forgive, divine."

—Alexander Pope

Life can throw a number of things at us in a short span of time.

For this exercise, imagine you're an oak tree rooted to the ground season after season. Throughout the stormy cycles or periods of change, what keeps you stable and rooted in your own life?

_____

_____

_____

_____

_____

_____

_____

_____

_____

_____

_____

_____

_____

_____

_____

_____

_____

_____

_____

_____

Where do you find inspiration in the world around you?

The smell of freshly baked cookies, a crackling campfire, the gentle patter of rain against the window... List your three favorite sounds, your three favorite sights, and your three favorite scents.

SOUNDS: _____
_____
_____
_____
_____
_____
_____

SIGHTS: _____
_____
_____
_____
_____
_____

SCENTS: _____
_____
_____
_____
_____
_____
_____

How do you feel after writing about your favorite things? Describe your emotions before and after completing the previous prompt.

One of the best ways to extend grace to others is to accept people fully for who they are.

Write about someone close to you with whom you don't always agree. How can you accept them for who they are, including their actions and their decisions?

_____

_____

_____

_____

_____

_____

_____

_____

_____

_____

_____

_____

_____

_____

_____

_____

_____

_____

_____

_____

Be a force of kindness.

List ten people you see every week—anyone ranging from family members to grocery store cashiers—and what you can say to build them up and make them feel better after seeing you.

1. _____

_____

2. _____

_____

3. _____

_____

4. _____

_____

5. _____

_____

6. _____

_____

7. _____

_____

8. _____

_____

9. _____

_____

10. _____

_____

_____

"People will never forget how you made them feel."

—Maya Angelou

You know that voice in your head? The one that's always criticizing you?

Give it a name and tell it how it makes you feel. It might feel silly to call that voice "Sad Sally" or "Negative Ned," but this exercise can help you identify and stop negative self-talk. Write to your inner critic here.

Have you ever felt personally responsible for something that happened, even if you had nothing to do with the situation?

That's called personalization, and it's just one of many types of negative thinking that can distort reality and rob you of happiness. Write about a time when you experienced personalization.

In this example, how could you have chosen grace instead?

In today's fast-paced, media-driven world, we are surrounded by messages and images that tell us we don't measure up, we're not doing enough, or that we can be better physically or financially.

How do these messages affect you, in both subtle and not-so-subtle ways? How can you block them out and focus on what really matters to you?

Feedback is important to help us grow—in our jobs, in our relationships, and in our lives.

But sometimes, we can shut down or become defensive when we hear criticism. Worse, we can internalize negative comments in a destructive way.

When was the last time you received negative feedback? How did it make you feel, and how did it affect your day?

How can you learn to process these types of comments while being kind to yourself?

Close your eyes and scan your body. Do you feel tension anywhere—in your forehead, shoulders, stomach, or elsewhere?

Take a deep breath, hold it for a count of five, and exhale. What are you holding on to that you can let go of right now?

"When I let go of what I am, I become what I might be."

—Lao Tzu

It can be challenging to focus on positives when fear speaks so much louder, but it's important to remember the good as well as the bad.

What are three things that made you smile this week? They can be any scale, big or small. Write about them here.

1. _____

_____

_____

_____

_____

_____

_____

_____

_____

_____

_____

_____

_____

_____

_____

_____

_____

_____

2. _____

3. _____

Negative words can create negative feelings. If words are getting you down, try flipping the script.

Fill in the negative blanks below, and then reframe them with a positive spin.

I HATE... _____

_____

_____

_____

POSITIVE FLIP: _____

_____

_____

_____

I CAN'T... _____

_____

_____

_____

POSITIVE FLIP: _____

_____

_____

_____

I WON'T... _____

_____

_____

POSITIVE FLIP: _____

_____

_____

I SHOULD HAVE . . . _____

_____

_____

_____

_____

POSITIVE FLIP: _____

_____

_____

_____

_____

I'LL NEVER BE ABLE TO . . . _____

_____

_____

_____

_____

POSITIVE FLIP: _____

_____

_____

_____

_____

I MISSED MY CHANCE TO . . . _____

_____

_____

_____

_____

POSITIVE FLIP: _____

_____

_____

_____

Sometimes, when an upcoming task or obstacle feels overwhelming, we forget that we're capable of handling it.

Identify one thing that's causing you stress. Which of your strengths does it play to? What skill do you have that will help you get this task done?

"The ideal person bears the accidents of life with dignity and grace, making the best of circumstances."

—Aristotle

Who can you turn to when you really need support?

List those people and why you can lean on them here.

PERSON 1: _____
_____
_____

WHY I CAN LEAN ON THEM: _____
_____
_____
_____
_____
_____
_____
_____

PERSON 2: _____
_____
_____

WHY I CAN LEAN ON THEM: _____
_____
_____
_____
_____
_____
_____
_____

PERSON 3: _____

_____

_____

WHY I CAN LEAN ON THEM: _____

_____

_____

_____

_____

_____

_____

_____

_____

PERSON 4: _____

_____

_____

WHY I CAN LEAN ON THEM: _____

_____

_____

_____

_____

_____

_____

_____

_____

_____

_____

Music is a powerful tool to help you tap into positive emotions and cultivate calm.

Draft your grace-full playlist here.

	Song	Artist
1.		
2.		
3.		
4.		
5.		
6.		
7.		
8.		
9.		
10.		
11.		

"One good thing about music is that when it hits you, you feel no pain."

—Bob Marley

What activities help you feel peaceful?

Make room for grace by scheduling feel-good, centering activities throughout the week. Write down one activity per day and when you'll commit to doing it.

MONDAY
ACTIVITY: _____
_____
_____
_____
_____
_____

SCHEDULED TIME: _____

TUESDAY
ACTIVITY: _____
_____
_____
_____

SCHEDULED TIME: _____

WEDNESDAY
ACTIVITY: _____
_____
_____

SCHEDULED TIME: _____

THURSDAY

ACTIVITY: _____

_____

_____

_____

_____

SCHEDULED TIME: _____

FRIDAY

ACTIVITY: _____

_____

_____

_____

_____

SCHEDULED TIME: _____

SATURDAY

ACTIVITY: _____

_____

_____

_____

SCHEDULED TIME: _____

SUNDAY

ACTIVITY: _____

_____

_____

_____

SCHEDULED TIME: _____

Take ten minutes to go outside and take a meditative walk.

Breathe fresh air and calmly take in your surroundings. What beauty did you notice?

_____

_____

_____

_____

_____

_____

_____

_____

_____

_____

_____

_____

_____

_____

_____

_____

_____

_____

_____

_____

_____

Practice taking feedback with grace.

Ask a family member or friend to give you their honest opinion. Write down their answers to the following questions.

How would you describe me as a [family member/friend]?

_____
_____
_____
_____
_____
_____
_____
_____
_____
_____
_____
_____
_____
_____
_____
_____
_____
_____
_____
_____
_____

What can I do to better our relationship?

Everyone has heard about random acts of kindness, but what about planned acts of kindness?

Strategize about how you can put some positivity into the world by brainstorming a list of small, daily acts of kindness you can do this week. Check them off once they're complete.

○ **MONDAY** _____
_____
_____
_____
_____
_____
_____
_____

○ **TUESDAY** _____
_____
_____
_____
_____
_____
_____
_____

○ **WEDNESDAY** _____
_____
_____
_____
_____

○ THURSDAY _____

_____
_____
_____
_____
_____
_____

○ FRIDAY _____

_____
_____
_____
_____
_____
_____

○ SATURDAY _____

_____
_____
_____
_____
_____
_____

○ SUNDAY _____

_____
_____
_____
_____

What's making you feel anxious right now?

What advice would a loved one give to help or comfort you?

_____

_____

_____

_____

_____

_____

_____

_____

_____

_____

_____

_____

_____

_____

_____

_____

_____

_____

_____

_____

_____

_____

_____

_____

_____

_____

_____

What's one unrealistic expectation you had for yourself today? How can you reframe it to be something that's achievable?

Example:

Unrealistic expectation: *I'm going to get everything on my to-do list done.*

Actually achievable goal: *I'm going to focus on the most important item on my to-do list and get it done.*

Look back on the past week.

Describe three achievements you're proud of.

1. _____
   _____
   _____
   _____
   _____
   _____
   _____
   _____
   _____
   _____
   _____
   _____

2. _____
   _____
   _____
   _____
   _____
   _____
   _____
   _____
   _____
   _____
   _____
   _____
   _____

3.

Bickering with a sibling. Disagreeing with a
parent. Debating with a colleague. Is there
someone who always gets a rise out of you?

Write about that person and the behavior pattern you fall
into with them; brainstorm ways you can break that pattern
for the both of you.

"Calmness is the cradle of power."

—Josiah Gilbert Holland

Social media can be a great tool for connecting with community, but it can also result in counting likes and comparing your life to others' posts.

Give yourself a break: step away from the socials for at least a few minutes every day. Plan a realistic social media time-out. What does it look like? How do you think it'll make you feel?

Helping others isn't only a kind thing to do, but it can help you get perspective on your problems.

Write down four volunteer opportunities. What about them would feel rewarding and fulfilling? What steps do you need to take to start helping?

1. _____
   _____
   _____
   _____
   _____
   _____
   _____
   _____
   _____
   _____

2. _____
   _____
   _____
   _____
   _____
   _____
   _____
   _____

3.

4.

Is that negative voice in your head too talkative these days?

Try this exercise: Write down every negative thought you have as it comes up today. At the end of the day, review what you've written. How do you feel, seeing all of those statements? What surprised you? How can you be kinder to yourself?

Try this exercise. Describe how you're feeling right now in the space provided.

_____

_____

_____

_____

_____

_____

_____

_____

_____

_____

_____

_____

_____

_____

_____

_____

_____

_____

_____

_____

Now, set a timer for ten minutes. Take a deep breath, close your eyes, and slowly repeat to yourself, "I choose grace for myself and for others." When the timer goes off, open your eyes.

How do you feel now? Is this an exercise you would try again?

Is it easier to offer compassion to yourself or to others? Why?

Think about a time when someone was patient with you.

You may have to reach back to childhood memories of a patient teacher, helping you learn a difficult concept, or it may be a recent conversation about a complex topic in the news.

Write about the person who was patient with you. How did their attention and unrushed demeanor make you feel? What did you learn from that moment?

_____

_____

_____

_____

_____

_____

_____

_____

_____

_____

_____

_____

_____

_____

_____

"Patience is a virtue.
Virtue is a grace."

—Proverb

Say the following words out loud, with conviction: *I am a good person.*

How did this make you feel? Did you feel lighter after saying those words? Did you cringe? Explore those feelings on these pages.

In general, why do you think forgiveness is so hard to come by?

_____

_____

_____

_____

_____

_____

_____

_____

_____

_____

_____

_____

_____

_____

_____

_____

_____

_____

_____

_____

_____

_____

_____

_____

_____

_____

Do you find it hard to forgive others? Is it hard to forgive yourself?

Sometimes you just need to laugh it off.

Write about a time when you couldn't stop laughing. What happened? How did you feel in the moment? How do you feel recalling it now?

_____

_____

_____

_____

_____

_____

_____

_____

_____

_____

_____

_____

_____

_____

_____

_____

_____

_____

_____

I should be further along in my career. I should have done better on that test. I should be able to run faster than I do.

The words *I should* are a cue that you're probably about to put yourself down. Write down all the *should* statements in your mind right now. Then be kind to yourself and draw a big X over the page.

I SHOULD . . . _____

_____

_____

_____

I SHOULD . . . _____

I SHOULD . . . _____

_____

_____

I SHOULD . . . _____

_____

I SHOULD . . . _____

_____

_____

I SHOULD . . . _____

I SHOULD . . . _____

_____

"You can never do kindness too soon, for you never know how soon it will be too late."

—Ralph Waldo Emerson

He's an old grouch. She's bossy. They are so disorganized. Beware of reducing others to labels.

At best, it's an oversimplification. At worst, it's dehumanizing. Write down some labeling statements you've used with others today. Then write a kinder statement about that person that acknowledges their human complexity.

_____

_____

_____

_____

_____

_____

_____

_____

_____

_____

_____

_____

_____

_____

_____

_____

_____

_____

Write about a time when someone truly
showed up for you in a difficult moment.

Who was it, and what did they do? How did their actions
make you feel?

How can you show up for them?

Self-care doesn't have to be complicated or time-consuming.

Set a timer for five minutes and go treat yourself. Need some ideas? Stretch. Meditate. Massage your own feet. Read a poem.

When the timer stops, write about what you did and how it felt to take five minutes for yourself.

_____

_____

_____

_____

_____

_____

_____

_____

_____

_____

_____

_____

_____

_____

_____

_____

_____

What are a few other five-minute self-care activities you can treat yourself with from time to time?

Getting your feelings down on paper can help
unburden your mind.

Write about something that feels overwhelming.

"People become attached to their burdens sometimes more than the burdens are attached to them."

—George Bernard Shaw

Being perfect is impossible—you're great just the way you are.

Write down ten ways you feel imperfect, and why that's just fine. For example: *My weight isn't great, but I've improved my fitness by committing to walking.*

1. _____
   _____
   _____
   _____
   _____

2. _____
   _____
   _____
   _____
   _____

3. _____
   _____
   _____
   _____
   _____

4. _____
   _____
   _____
   _____
   _____
   _____

5.

6.

7.

8.

9.

10.

Think about your best friend.

Write down how they make you feel about yourself. How can you be a friend to yourself in the same way?

Do you trust yourself?

Why or why not?

_____

_____

_____

_____

_____

_____

_____

_____

_____

_____

_____

_____

_____

_____

_____

_____

_____

_____

_____

_____

_____

_____

_____

What would it take for you to trust yourself more?

Who did you make smile today?

How did you do it?

"Use your smile to change the world; don't let the world change your smile."

—Proverb

What types of activities give you energy?
What drains your energy?

	Energy giving	Energy draining
1.		
2.		
3.		
4.		
5.		
6.		

How can you make more time for what energizes you?

Give yourself a day off.

Imagine you have twenty-four hours all to yourself—you have no responsibilities—and you can spend it any way you want. Fill in the schedule for your waking hours during the day. Then circle any activities you can do this week.

6:00 AM: _____

_____

7:00 AM: _____

_____

8:00 AM: _____

_____

9:00 AM: _____

_____

10:00 AM: _____

_____

11:00 AM: _____

_____

12:00 PM: _____

_____

1:00 PM: _____

_____

2:00 PM: _____

_____

3:00 PM: _____

_____

4:00 PM: _____

_____

5:00 PM: _____

_____

6:00 PM: _____

_____

7:00 PM: _____

_____

8:00 PM: _____

_____

9:00 PM: _____

_____

10:00 PM: _____

_____

11:00 PM: _____

_____

Fill these two pages completely with compliments about yourself and positive affirmations.

Don't stop until every line is filled.

_____
_____
_____
_____
_____
_____
_____
_____
_____
_____
_____
_____
_____
_____
_____
_____
_____
_____
_____
_____
_____

Write about a time when you faced your fears.

What happened? What did it feel like?

_____

_____

_____

_____

_____

_____

_____

_____

_____

_____

_____

_____

_____

_____

_____

_____

_____

_____

_____

_____

_____

_____

"Courage is grace
under pressure."

—Ernest Hemingway

Write down the best three compliments
people have ever given you.

Make sure to note who said it and when and how it made
you feel.

COMPLIMENT 1: _____

_____

_____

_____

_____

_____

_____

_____

PERSON: _____

_____

HOW I FELT: _____

_____

_____

_____

_____

_____

_____

_____

_____

_____

COMPLIMENT 2: _____

_____

_____

_____

_____

PERSON: _____

_____

HOW I FELT: _____

_____

_____

_____

_____

COMPLIMENT 3: _____

_____

_____

_____

_____

PERSON: _____

_____

HOW I FELT: _____

_____

_____

_____

_____

_____

Pen an uplifting note to someone you see every day.

Tell them why they matter to you, and how they make your life better. Provide as many details as possible.

DEAR _____ :

_____

_____

_____

_____

_____

_____

_____

_____

_____

_____

_____

_____

_____

_____

_____

_____

_____

_____

_____

_____

_____

Look back to page eight of this journal, where you wrote down what *grace* meant to you.

As you complete this book, has your answer changed? Why or why not?

Page back through what you've written in this journal.

How does it feel to see all the work you've done? How has choosing grace—for yourself and others—changed your life?

How do you hold on to grace?

"Will is to grace
as the horse is
to the rider."

—Saint Augustine